THE SECOND WORLD WAR

ANN WEBLEY

Chrysalis Children's Books

First published in the UK in 2005 by
Chrysalis Children's Books,
An imprint of Chrysalis Books Group,
The Chrysalis Building, Bramley Road, London W10 6SP

Associate Publisher: Joyce Bentley
Editor: Debbie Foy
Art director: Sarah Goodwin
Designer: Angie Allison
Illustrator: Peter Bailey

ISBN 1 84458 326 0

British Library Cataloguing in Publication Data for
this book is available from the British Library.

Printed in Great Britain by
Clays Ltd, St Ives plc

10 9 8 7 6 5 4 3 2 1

CONTENTS

THE SECOND WORLD WAR

Following the end of the First World War in 1918, Germany was punished for its part in the war and:
+ Had to pay other countries a lot of money;
+ Was not allowed to build up the armed forces (army, navy and air force);
+ Had some land taken away.

The German people were angry!

Life was hard in the 1930s:
+ People could not buy as much with their money;
+ Lots of people lost their jobs.

In 1933 Adolf Hitler, leader of the Nazi party, became the leader of Germany. He promised the German people that he would make the country strong again so he:
+ Re-armed Germany;
+ Invaded nearby countries because he said they were really meant to be part of Germany.

Other countries put up with Hitler's actions until he threatened Poland, but, in the meantime, they started getting ready for war.

Neville Chamberlain, Britain's Prime Minister at that time, said that if Poland was attacked, Britain would then go to war.

On **1 September 1939** Germany invaded Poland. Prime Minister Chamberlain stuck to his word and two days later – on **3 September 1939** – the Second World War began.

Almost as soon as war was declared, the air raid sirens went off in London! Everyone thought that London was being bombed – but luckily it was a false alarm!

Other countries soon got involved. Italy fought on the same side as Germany. Their leader was called Mussolini. Russia was on the same side as Britain and France. Their leader was called Stalin.

SOME IMPORTANT DATES DURING THE WAR

May/June 1940: Dunkirk landing – 'Operation Dynamo'.
The Germans trapped the British soldiers on the beach at
Dunkirk. A huge fleet of small boats came to rescue them.

May 1940: Hitler made plans to invade Britain. Winston Churchill
became Prime Minister.

June 1940: British and German planes fought over southern
England. Britain won the battle in the air.

1940 – 1941: The Blitz. German planes bombed British cities.
German cities were bombed as well.

1941: The Japanese, who were on the same side as Germany,
bombed Pearl Harbour – the United States Naval base in Hawaii.
As a result of this, USA joined the war on the side of Britain
and France.

1941 – 1944: The war was fought in Europe, North Africa, Japan
and Burma.

6th June 1944: D-Day. Allied troops landed on the Normandy
beaches in France – 'Operation Overlord'. They pushed back
the Germans.

7th May 1945: Germany surrendered.

8th May 1945: VE Day (Victory in Europe).

August 1945: America dropped two atomic bombs on the Japanese cities of Hiroshima and Nagasaki.

14th August 1945: VJ Day (Victory over Japan). Japan surrendered.

FAMOUS PEOPLE

You might like to find out more about these famous men and women.

Winston Churchill:

+ Led a 'coalition' government. This means that all political parties worked together because there was a war;
+ Was a great orator (speaker);
+ Wanted people to believe they could win the war;
+ Said it would be hard – it would take 'blood, toil, tears and sweat'.

King George VI and Queen Elizabeth:

+ Were very popular during the war because they chose to stay in London;
+ Said they could 'now look the East End (of London) in the face' when the palace was bombed.

Adolf Hitler:

+ Was born in Austria;
+ Was an artist who became a politician and then leader of Germany;
+ Was a great orator;
+ German people believed him when he said he would make Germany great again;
+ Shot himself when he realised Germany was going to lose the war.

Vera Lynn:

+ Was a singer who was called 'The Forces' Sweetheart';
+ Performed in shows put on to entertain the troops;
+ Sang songs like *We'll Meet Again* and *The White Cliffs of Dover* which made people feel proud to be fighting the war.

WHAT HAPPENED AT THE END OF THE WAR?

On VE Day, Winston Churchill spoke to the country on the radio – it was called the 'wireless' in those days. He then went on to the balcony at Buckingham palace with the King and Queen.

There were celebrations everywhere!

✦ Ships sounded their hooters when coming in to dock or leaving shore;

✦ People danced in the streets. They waved Union Jack flags and hung them patriotically at their windows;

✦ Church bells rang out – they had been silent during the war. They were only to be rung as a warning in case of a German invasion;

✦ Street parties were held all over the country. Long tables were put down the middle of streets and special food was prepared.

People were thrilled that the fighting and blackouts were finally over. However, it would be several years before the British people saw the end of food rationing (see pages 33–36).

Germany was divided. Even Berlin – the capital of Germany – was divided. East Berlin was separated from West Berlin by the Berlin Wall.

The four allies – Britain, France, USA and Russia – each controlled a section of Germany after the war. Britain, France and USA did not really trust Russia once the war had ended so there was a lot more trouble to come.

Today, Germany is part of the European Union and is friendly with Britain. The Berlin Wall was finally pulled down in 1989.

On 11 November each year, people wear poppies to remember the people who died in the two world wars.

The Second World War changed people's lives and they never forgot what happened.

ALBERT'S WAR

My name is Albert. In 1939 I was living in east London with my Mum and Dad.

3 September 1939 – 11.15am: that was a time everyone remembers. The Prime Minister, Neville Chamberlain, came on the wireless and said that we were at war with Germany. He told everyone that he thought it would have been possible to sort everything out but that Hitler wasn't interested. After he had spoken, there were lots of announcements about what was going to happen and the work people might have to do.

Not long after that Dad had a medical to make sure he was fit and then he went off to training camp.

On 1 September 1939, a new law said that all men between the ages of 18 and 40 could be called up to fight. This was called 'conscription'. Men joined the army, the navy or the air force.

In 1941, the law was changed as more people were needed to fight:
✦ Men up to the age of 51 could be conscripted or 'called up';
✦ Britain became the first country to call women for war work. Single women between 20 and 30 could be conscripted – though they did not fight.

We had all been really scared when the air raid siren went as soon as the war started. Before he went, Dad turned our dining room table into a proper Morrison shelter. As you can see, there was wire and mesh around the sides of the table and a mattress underneath.

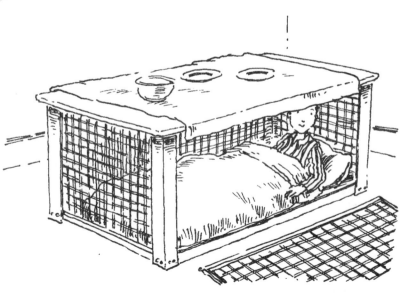

Many people had Anderson shelters in their garden. The government gave millions of these away to people because they provided good protection in an air raid.

The Anderson shelter was made of corrugated steel and it had to be sunk nearly a metre into the ground. It was then covered with a layer of earth, about 45cm thick. Some people grew vegetables on the top of their shelter! The shelters were about the size of a small shed. People lit them with torches, candles or oil lamps. They put bedding inside so they would be ready if they had to get out of their houses during the night.

Some people in our street didn't make a Morrison shelter. They hid in the cupboard under the stairs. There are some flats about a mile away and they didn't have any shelters either so everyone used to crouch down in the stair wells. I wouldn't have liked that much!

In London, people began to use the underground stations as shelters. During the Blitz, many people went straight to the stations after work and slept on the platforms each night. Some people even managed to organise bunks and sometimes

food was provided. At Christmas, people put up decorations. Many people preferred to go to the stations, even though it was further from home. They felt safer because they were deeper underground and this also made it quieter.

Before the war started, everyone in Britain was given a gas mask by the government. This was mine. We were shown how to use it at school. Sometimes we even did our lessons wearing the mask so that we could get used to it. We didn't get much work done though. It was made of very smelly rubber and and the glass had a habit of steaming up all the time. The best bit about wearing a gas mask was blowing 'raspberry' noises when we breathed out!

Like the child's mask, the basic adult mask also had pieces of charcoal and cotton wool inside a filter. This let clean air in but kept harmful gas out. People gave the masks different names such as 'dickey birds' (because they looked as though they had beaks), 'canaries', 'Hitlers' or 'nosebags'.

There was a special mask in a bag for babies and you could even get one for your dog.

Luckily, there was never a gas attack during the war.

During the war there was a blackout. This wasn't just in the cities. It was in the countryside as well. The idea was to stop the Germans finding their way if they came at night. They wouldn't be able to find their targets. There were rules we had to follow. This is what we had to do at home:

✦ *Cover our windows with heavy material if there was a light on inside;*

  ✦ *Turn out all the lights before we opened the door.*

Some people got fed up with putting up the blackout every night and painted over their windows or used cardboard or thick paper to cover them. This often happened in factories and this meant that windows could not be opened during the day. Workers complained that the factories were very stuffy. One of the jobs of the air raid wardens was to check that no lights from windows (or anywhere else) were showing. They would shout: 'Put out that light!' whenever they saw a gap that let some light through.

A government information leaflet said:

'When you first come into the blackout, stand still for a minute and get your eyes used to the darkness.'

It was black as soot out in the streets during the war. There were no street lights or traffic lights. You had to cover up the lights on cars and bikes except for a thin strip down the middle. Buses and trains had blinds fixed to the windows. We were told to carry a white handkerchief if we went out. That way we might be seen!

Although there were fewer cars on the streets because people could not get petrol, there were a lot of accidents due to the blackout.

Later in the war, the tops of pillar boxes were painted green or yellow. This was because drops of deadly mustard gas would stain the paint and show up if there was a gas attack. In addition, some white lines were painted on kerbs and this helped safety a little.

Mum and Dad told me that there were plans to get children out of the cities even before the war started. In September 1939 the evacuation started and:

✦ *Children older than 5 were evacuated with their teachers;*

✦ *Younger children were evacuated with their mothers or stayed behind.*

I didn't go with the first lot of evacuees. I only went later when the bombing got really bad. I went to the station with some others. We all had labels on as though we were parcels. Mine said 'Albert Smith. St. John's Junior School.' I had a small case carrying my clothes and a couple of books, and my gas mask was in a cardboard box.

Thousands of children were evacuated at the start of the war. However, a lot of them returned. This was partly due to the fact that the air raids did not start at the beginning of the war as everyone expected. It was also because many were unhappy and homesick in the countryside.

A government propaganda poster tried to persuade mothers not to let their children return. It showed a ghostly figure of Hitler behind a mother and child saying, 'Take them back' but the message on the poster is: 'Don't do it Mother – leave the children where they are.'

I was still in London during some of the bombing. The first planes usually dropped firebombs so they could see by the light of the fires. The air raid wardens rushed about trying to put the fires out as fast as they could. The air raid siren would start and everyone made for shelter. In the morning we would go out to look at the damage. Whole streets got flattened some nights.

The Blitz began at 5pm on 7 September 1940. Six hundred German bombers flew over the city targeting gas stations, power stations and the docks. Raids went on night after night. One of the worst raids was on Sunday 29 December 1940. Two eyewitnesses described the scene:

'The whole of London seemed alight! We were hemmed in by a wall of flame in every direction.'

'The air felt singed. I was breathing ashes … The air itself, as we walked, smelt of burning.'

Raids continued on and off during 1941. While Albert was in the country, London faced two more threats.

In June 1944, Germany sent pilotless jet planes during the daytime. These carried a bomb known as the V1, also called the 'Doodlebug' or the 'Flying Bomb'. People first heard the sharp buzzing of the engine. Then there was a sudden silence as the engine cut out and the bomb fell to the ground. Londoners used to hold their breath and pray that the plane would pass over.

In August 1944, the V2 (Vengeance 2) rocket attacked London. This was a long distance rocket that could travel about 3,000 miles an hour. There was no warning. The first one hit Chiswick in West London and the explosion was heard seven miles away. Many buildings were completely destroyed.

November 1940 ▓▓▓▓▓▓▓▓▓▓▓*

Dear Albert,

I hope you are getting on well in Devon. I'm sorry I haven't been able to write to you for a while but things have been very difficult.

I don't know how much you've read in the newspapers. My regiment has been fighting in France but we got pushed further and further back. In the end we were trapped in a small area in northern France near Dunkirk. The German army was coming and I knew this was the end if something amazing didn't happen soon.

Well something amazing did! On May 27th we spotted some boats sailing towards us. There were all kinds, fishing boats, pleasure boats – nothing big because they would never have got up to the beaches. German bombers were going over all the time and lots of men didn't make it. I was one of the lucky ones.

Later we went to ▓▓▓▓▓▓▓▓▓▓▓▓▓▓▓▓▓▓▓▓▓▓▓ ▓▓▓▓▓▓▓▓▓▓▓▓▓▓▓▓▓▓▓▓▓▓▓▓ I think about you all the time and long for the end of this war.

Lots of love
Dad

*THE CENSOR BLACKED OUT ANYTHING IN A LETTER THAT MIGHT HELP THE ENEMY.

Between 27 May and 4 June 1940, 338,226 people were rescued from the beaches at Dunkirk. It was known as the 'Dunkirk landing'. Ordinary people who owned boats had listened to a radio appeal to help rescue the soldiers and they had come out in force.

GEORGE'S WAR

My name is George. My Mum and Dad run the grocer's shop in a small town in Devon. Dad joined the navy at the start of the war so Mum worked in the shop by herself and I often helped her.

We got some evacuees as soon as the war started. They came from London and also from places like Southampton, Sheffield and other big cities. These were places that the Germans were bombing hard.

We had a billeting officer like all the other towns that had evacuees. It was her job to sort out somewhere for them all to stay. Once a whole lot arrived at once and they were all taken to the village hall. People went down to choose who to have. Other times, only a few came and Mrs. Smedley came knocking on doors and tried to persuade people to have another city kid. She had a rotten job because no-one wanted them.

How did the war affect me? Well in lots of ways, of course, but I'll tell you three things:

1. Someone made rules about the clothes we wore. I had to wear short trousers all the time to save material. You were only allowed to wear long trousers when you were 12.

2. One rotten thing was that sweets were rationed and so we could only get a very small amount.

3. But one thing I didn't mind was being told I couldn't have as many baths as usual! There was even a rule about how deep the bath water could be – so that the water wouldn't be wasted. We had to paint a line round the sides of the bath so that we knew when the water reached 5 inches [about 12cm] deep. Having a bath could be pretty chilly!

All the kids in the town got involved in helping the war effort. The scouts and guides were always organising things and helping to raise money. They also ran a messenger service in the local area and pedalled about on their bikes.

I was in the 'cogs'. We went round collecting salvage – that's anything that could be turned into something useful to help win the war.

We collected:
- *Rubber*
- *Saucepans*
- *Kettles*
- *Rags*
- *Animal bones*
- *Waste paper*
- *Tin baths and old tin cans*
- *Toothpaste tubes*

We went round the streets with barrows singing 'There'll always be a dustbin' to the tune of 'There'll always be an England'.

The items collected were used to make parts for planes, ships, guns and bombs. All new metal and rubber produced had to be used to make weapons. Metal items for the home were hard to find in shops!

The government started something called 'Dig for Victory'. The idea was to make sure that we never ran out of food. We had to use any bit of ground to grow vegetables so we started to grow potatoes, carrots and parsnips in our small garden.

Teams of mothers and children cleared waste land for planting. As they did so, they collected nettles. These tasted a bit like spinach when they were boiled.

Two of the men on Newton's farm left to go and fight. Someone sent two 'land girls'. They did all the jobs the men had done.

The 'land girls' were the Women's Land Army. They were given a uniform and lived either in the farmhouse or a nearby hostel. They worked up to 14 hours a day doing the milking, ploughing, tree felling or anything else that was needed. It was hard work but was a more healthy life than working in a factory.

In the holidays and at very busy times my friends from school would go over and do all sorts of jobs to help. 'Lend a hand on the land' was what everyone said.

Our town had a branch of the Local Defence Volunteers. These were blokes who were too old to join up or who hadn't passed the medical. They soon became known as the Home Guard and their job was to make sure that the area was safe from attack if the Germans landed. The Home Guard also took down all the signposts around our town and painted out any sign on a shop that said the name of the town. This was so the enemy would get lost if they got this far. I don't know about the enemy, but people here got lost plenty of times! The station sign was taken down as well.

The Home Guard were given uniforms and weapons and some training. They were not paid. Some of them were quite elderly men who wanted to do something to help their town. They held regular meetings and organised expeditions to practise. People would see columns of home guard troops patrolling the countryside, checking for spies or enemy troops. They would take it in turns to play the part of a German soldier.

There were GIs (American soldiers) in the camp a few miles away during the war. We used to see them in the town when they had time off. They gave us sweets – but they called it candy – and they also had something I'd not tried before, chewing gum.

The first American soldiers arrived in Britain in January 1942. The British called them GIs because all their packs and equipment had labels on saying 'GI Government Issue'. They were also called 'yanks'. The American soldiers had more money than the British and they were quite generous, giving away not only sweets and gum but also nylon stockings and lipstick to the girls.

The American soldiers were given information about the British people before they came. One page said: 'You will soon find yourself among a kindly, quiet, hard-working people who have been living under a strain such as few people in the world have ever known.'

School was a bit different during the war. The school also got crammed with all the evacuee children and their teachers. The classes were bigger and we ran out of everything we needed.

We did lots of fundraising at school to help the war effort. Once we organised a concert and all our families came to watch us. We sent the money to the Navy because one of our teachers, Mr. Brown, had gone to join a ship. We got a letter back thanking us which was very nice because they must have been rather busy.

Many schools closed as teachers joined up and by January 1940 a third of children had no permanent school. Some schools were so full that they organised a shift system with different children going in at different times.

In towns, brick bomb-blast doors were built in front of school entrances. Windows were criss-crossed with sticky tape to stop flying glass. School playing fields were used to anchor barrage balloons. They floated high in the sky and were supposed to keep German planes away. Children practised for air raids during school time.

Coughs and sneezes spread diseases

Our teachers talked to us about the war. They showed us lots of posters that the government had made to tell us what to do. This one used to get on my nerves because our teachers and parents used to chant 'Coughs and sneezes spread diseases' all the time!

I liked this one. It's about not talking in case you give secrets away. We used to play games and pretend to be German spies and British soldiers!

"Of course there's no harm in *your* knowing!"

CARELESS TALK COSTS LIVES

People also listened to the *Nine o'clock news* but were not always told everything that was going on.

There weren't many new toys around during the war. We used to play with our gas masks quite a lot. If you held onto the strap, you could swing it round your head like a weapon. The person with the most dents in their mask was the champion. We got into trouble for playing that because it damaged the gas mask.

Another game we played was called 'plonk' – this was like darts but it had a different board. The highest score was 100 points into the open mouth of Hitler!

One thing we all enjoyed doing was listening to the wireless. There were two channels: the Home Service which had news of the war and serious programmes and the Forces Programme which had music and comedy shows. One of our favourites was ITMA. That stood for 'It's That Man Again' and was the comedian Tommy Handley. He was really good at coming up with quick jokes to make everyone laugh. One thing he said that always made Mum laugh was NKABTYSITRWU which meant 'Never Kiss A Baby Till You're Sure It's The Right Way Up!' The programme ended with Tommy Handley saying TTFN – 'Ta Ta For Now'. People used to go round saying all these catch phrases to each other. Mum's favourite film was The Goose Steps Out. *Will Hay made fun of Hitler and everyone enjoyed that!*

The Germans also broadcast programmes which were especially for the British. A traitor with an upper class accent spoke on the radio and tried to make the people give up. However, no-one believed him and he became a family joke. People called him 'Lord Haw-Haw'.

MAVIS AND JOAN'S WAR

I'm Joan, George's Mum. I run the grocer's shop in the high street in Little Poppleton.

I'm Mavis, Albert's Mum. I live in London and after Albert went to the country, I started work in a factory.

We both had to get used to rationing during the war. It was to make sure there was food to go round. Everyone had a ration book – even the King and Queen!

Everyone had to register with a grocer and a butcher and you always had to do your shopping at the same place. I have to cut the coupons out of the book when people buy food that is rationed.

These are the sorts of amounts that one person is allowed for a week:

+ *4oz (100g) cheese*
+ *4oz (100g) bacon*
+ *2oz (50g) butter*
+ *2oz (50g) cooking fat*
+ *2oz (50g) margarine*
+ *8oz (200g) sugar*
+ *4oz (100g) jam*
+ *2oz (50g) tea – for adults*
+ *1 egg – 3 for children*
+ *3 eggs as dried egg powder*
+ *7 pints of milk for children under 5*
+ *3½ pints of milk for school age children*
+ *1 pint's worth of dried milk*
+ *¾lb (350g) minced beef – or other meat to the same value*

1 Egg   4oz cheese   a glass of milk   4oz Bacon

Fresh food like fish, bread and offal (liver and kidneys) wasn't rationed. Nor was fruit, but it was often very hard to get. You had to queue up for things in short supply. I hardly saw a banana during the war and oranges were kept for the children.

There were plenty of vegetables around during the war. We used to make a vegetable pie called 'Woolton pie', named after the Minister of Food.

Jam and cakes were made from carrots. We had to get used to dry milk and dried eggs. I never liked the dried egg powder – it made very rubbery omelettes.

Since sugar was in short supply, people were not allowed to ice cakes. They hired cardboard covers, made to look like icing, for wedding cakes. Rationing on many sweets carried on after the war and did not end until 1953.

Although food was in such short supply, people were generally healthy during the war. They ate lots of vegetables and no-one over-ate due to the rationing system!

There was always a lot of advice about recipes in newspapers and magazines and on the wireless.

Here are some things we tried:
- *Raw sprouts and cabbage in salads;*
- *A kind of coffee made from ground acorns;*
- *Carrot marmalade;*
- *Grated raw beetroot in cakes instead of dried fruit;*
- *A 'banana' sandwich – cooled, cooked parsnip flavoured with artificial banana flavouring.*

It was important that people tried as many things as possible. Any food that could not be produced in this country had to be brought in by ship. The German navy was trying to sink the ships and that put the sailors' lives at risk. This meant that only really necessary items were brought in from other countries.

> *Why not try my recipe for carrot pudding? It was one of our favourites during the war.*
>
> *1 cup of breadcrumbs* *1 cup of dried fruit*
> *1 cup of grated carrot* *1 cup of grated potato*
> *1 teaspoon of bicarbonate of soda* *2 teaspoons of hot water*
>
> *Put all the ingredients into a bowl and mix them together. Turn the mixture into a pudding basin and cover it with greaseproof paper. Cook for approximately 2 hours over boiling water, making sure that it doesn't boil dry.*

There were some ways to get extra food.

Shopkeepers kept supplies of unrationed food off the shelves and only sold it to their regular customers. This was called 'under the counter' and the shopkeepers had to charge the price fixed by the government. Most ordinary people did buy things this way. However, only the rich could afford to buy items on the 'black market'. This meant that they paid a high price to get items that were scarce. It was illegal to sell things in this way.

Extra rations were introduced in November 1941. People were allowed an extra 16 'points' a month. They could choose to buy a luxury-type food such as biscuits, dried fruit, breakfast cereals and tinned food. However, very often some foods on the points system were not available and people would just have to take whatever foods were available.

There were often long queues in high streets and sometimes people queued up for goods without knowing what the queues were for!

We also had ration books for clothes. In 1940 everyone was allowed 60 coupons, though later this was reduced to 48. For example:

Number of coupons:
- Woman's coat – 14
- Dress – 11
- Jumper (child) – 3
- Handkerchief – ½
- Man's coat – 16
- Pair of shoes (child) – 5
- Gloves – 2

There were all sorts of rules as well:
- Men's suits could only have three pockets and three buttons on the front;
- No fancy belts;
- Trouser legs couldn't be wider than 19 inches [45cm];
- No elastic waistbands or turn-ups in trousers;
- No pleats in skirts because they wasted material.

All through the war, propaganda posters told us to 'Make do and mend' and we got quite good at it.
- We made new clothes out of old ones that children had outgrown;
- We turned a dress into a skirt and a blouse;
- We melted down old lipsticks to make new ones and used soot for eye shadow;
- Ladies stockings were in short supply so we sometimes painted our legs with gravy browning and pencilled a line down the back to look like the seam.

In some areas, women got together once a week to knit socks, jumpers, hats and scarves for the men at war.

Food and clothes were not the only things in short supply. It was hard to get:

♦ Crockery and cutlery;   ♦ Towels;
♦ Blankets and pillows;   ♦ Furniture;
♦ Buckets;   ♦ Toys.

Soap for washing and cleaning the house and clothes was rationed.

One of the characters we got used to seeing on posters was the 'Squanderbug'.

People were persuaded not to waste anything because if we did we were helping Hitler.

Not many people had cars during the war. Petrol was rationed because it was needed for the armed forces. Propaganda posters also tried to persuade people not to travel about too much.

My husband is a grocer and Mavis's husband is a locksmith.

They both had to join up. But some people were doing very important jobs and these were called 'reserved occupations'. Those people were not conscripted because their job was considered important for the war effort.

Examples of reserve occupations were farmers, train drivers, policemen, and some civil servants who worked for the government. At first, they were allowed to join up so many of them did. This caused a problem and certain jobs became EWO (Essential Work Order). People in these jobs could not be sacked and they could not leave their jobs even if they wanted to.

When my husband, Harold, went to war I wanted to help the war effort. When Albert went to the country, I started work in a factory that made weapons. Just think! Harold might have used a weapon I made! I had a long journey across London each day to get there and then worked ten hours. We did shift work so sometimes I worked at night. It was horrible travelling through the blackout to get to work.

Over three million men were away in the armed forces and this
meant that there were lots of jobs that had to be done by women.
Single women were conscripted for this work but married women
could also volunteer. At first, many factory owners doubted whether
the women would be able to do what was needed but they were
proved wrong. This was a very big change for women because in
those days most women stopped work when they got married.

All over the country women put together weapons and bombs,
made parts for aeroplanes, worked on the railways, drove trucks and
did many other jobs that had previously only been done by men.
Many factories changed their products during the war. Chocolate
and cosmetic factories, for example, started to make war items.
Other women, who did not work in factories, joined the WVS –

Women's Voluntary Service. They ran soldiers' tea bars, rolled bandages for hospitals and did a host of other jobs to help the war effort. Some women joined the services, for example the Women's Royal Naval Service (also known as the WRENS) but they were not allowed to fight.

We wouldn't like you to think it was all bad. We had a lot of fun in London during the war. There were lots of songs written to keep everyone cheerful and we were always having sing-songs.

We went to dances and the Big Bands played all the popular tunes. One new dance was called 'The Blackout Stroll'. After doing some steps, the lights would go out and we all had to change partners in the dark! It was a lot of fun.

We also went to the cinema and the theatre. The Windmill Theatre in the West End kept going right through the Blitz. War films were the favourites and, of course, the British always won!

No-one had televisions during the war but when they went to the cinema they saw *Pathe News*. This was a newsreel about what was happening in other countries.

Reading was popular but books were printed on special paper called 'austerity paper'.

Most of the usual sports stopped in the war. There was no first class football, rugby or cricket to go and watch.

INTO THE DRAMA

IINTRODUCTION

You know a lot about life during the Second World War now so you can prepare for the play. You could work as a group and act it out as it is written. Or you could also become playwrights yourselves by adding new characters or scenes.

Whichever you choose, there are a lot of jobs for people in your group and you will probably have more than one thing to do!

You need people in charge of:
+ Costumes;
+ Sets;
+ Props;
+ Designing a programme;
+ Music.

You will also need:
+ Actors;
+ A producer (someone who is in charge of putting the whole play together);
+ Writers (if you intend to add to the play).

Read on to get lots of ideas!

HOW TO WRITE A PLAY

✦ Start each scene by describing where the characters are with details of the time of day and the weather if those are important. Write this in the present tense. eg **September 1940, the dining room of the Smith house in London.**

✦ Write the names of the characters on the left hand side of the page and use a colon to introduce what they say. eg **ALFRED:**

✦ Never use speech marks or speech verbs in a play.

✦ Use character direction only when necessary. Put this in brackets or a different colour before, during or after the speech. This shows how the words are said and helps to bring the characters to life. eg **ALFRED: (sounding upset)**.

✦ Think hard about the characters and make their personalities come through in what they say. Make sure they 'stay in character'. Use stage directions to move the plot along and show what the characters do during the scene. eg **They get out from under the table. Harold goes out the door. Mavis and Albert clear the table.**

✦ Different colours or fonts can be used to separate the different parts of the writing.

✦ Only use a narrator if it is really necessary.

How To Add To The Play

1. Add to a scene

A character could tell the others about:

✦ Going to a dance at a bigger town;

✦ Getting into trouble for not having blackout up at a window.

2. Include more characters

For example:

✦ Other children – either country children or evacuees;

✦ A butcher;

✦ Shoppers;

✦ Some Americans.

3. Add a scene

You could extend the play by:

✦ Adding a scene at the school – when they are sorting the salvage or practising for the concert;

✦ Adding a scene early in the war when Mavis comes to visit Albert.

4. Write another play with the same characters

Here is one idea:

✦ Write a play consisting of more than one scene that is set at Christmas – think about how it would be different in war time.

5. Change the ending

✦ You might decide that your play will not have such a happy ending so you could re-write scene 6.

HOW TO MAKE YOUR NEW PLAY REALISTIC

Use detail from life during the Second World War

If you look carefully at the play in chapter 6 you will get a good idea of how to make your play realistic.

Notice how detail about changes to everyday life comes in:
✦ The setting – detail about the Blitz and the blackout;
✦ The jobs people do;
✦ Things that happened during the war. The play starts with the family listening to Chamberlain's speech.

If you add to the play, you will be able to use more information from chapters 2, 3 and 4 as well as detail from books in your class or school library.

Use words and expressions used during the war

There were a great many words and expressions used and they varied according to where people lived.

Here is some wartime slang:

✦ Pit = bed;
✦ Kerdumf = crash;
✦ Solid = stupid;
✦ Niff-naff = fuss;
✦ Pan = face;
✦ Rabbits = smuggled goods;
✦ Bolo = mad;

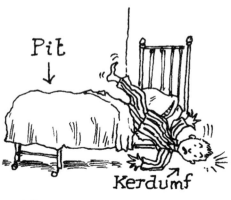

- ✦ Sardine tin = submarine;
- ✦ Beer trap = mouth;
- ✦ Buckshee = free;
- ✦ Akka = money;
- ✦ Schooly = a teacher who joined the army.

Sardine tin

There were also many abbreviations used:

- ✦ RAF = Royal Air Force;
- ✦ WVS = Women's Voluntary Service;
- ✦ POW = Prisoner of war;
- ✦ AWOL = Absent without leave;
- ✦ GI = American soldier – 'General Issue'.

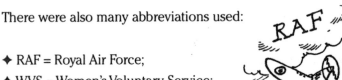

Add music

Music was very popular during the Second World War. People listened to the radio, went to concerts and enjoyed singing well known songs to keep their spirits up.

The words of the songs were about England winning the war and being united in times of trouble. You should be able to find the words and music easily if you decide to include it in your play.

Some of the most popular were:

Run rabbit run

- ✦ *There'll always be an England;*
- ✦ *We'll meet again;*
- ✦ *When you're up to your neck in hot water, be like a kettle and sing;*

◆ *Run rabbit run;*
◆ *In the quartermaster stores;*
◆ *We're going to hang out the washing on the Siegfried line.*

The 'Siegfried line' was a line of German fortification in Europe.
The English made fun of it by saying they would hang their washing
on the line. This showed that they did not take it very seriously.

Include some wartime verses

These were written to get a message across to people easily.
The idea was that if they remembered the poem, they would
remember the message.

When fisher folk are brave enough
To face the mines and foe for you;
You surely can be bold enough
To try a kind of fish that's new.

If you've news of our munitions
Keep it dark.
Ships or planes or troop positions
Keep it dark.
Lives are lost through conversation
Here's a tip for the duration
When you've private information
Keep it dark!

This song is from an advertisement for wool:

There's more that goes to win a war
Than tanks and planes and guns!
Than men prepared to do their best
To overthrow the Huns.

The Home Front too must play its part
And you can do your bit
To help our gallant fighting lads
By starting now – to knit!

You cannot knit too many things
To keep out wet and cold;
Like mittens, helmets, socks and scarves
Go to it – young and old!

GETTING READY FOR THE PERFORMANCE

1. Introduction

You are nearly ready. You have practised the play and maybe added your own characters or scenes.

You might be going to perform:

+ To the class;
+ To the school;
+ To your parents.

Depending on who your audience is and where you are going to perform, you'll need to decide about sets, props and costumes. This can be as simple or as complicated as you like.

2. Costumes

+ The simplest way to show a character is to get them to wear one item. For example, Mavis could wear an apron and the boys could wear caps.

+ If you want to dress people properly use:

- Shirts and short grey trousers for boys;
- Blouses and straight, knee-length skirt for girls (they saved material by having straight styles);
- Little cardigans and V-necked pullovers.

You don't have to be good at sewing. Staples and glue can alter clothes quickly – but make sure you get an adult's permission before you start!

3. Sets

Once again, this can be very simple or much more complicated.

✦ The simplest way is to make a frame and stand different labels against it which tell the audience where the characters are. For example: **Scene 1: The Smith's dining room in London.** Use tables and chairs in your classroom for any furniture needed.

✦ If you are using a stage, you could paint a setting onto a white sheet or a roll of corrugated paper. This can be fixed up behind the actors. You will need people to change the sheet for each new scene. Look at pictures in the books in your classroom and then compare them with the scenes in the play. This will help you decide what to paint.

4. Props

You need to collect the objects the actors are going to use. It is hard to 'pretend' to swap cigarette cards. It is better to cut up some pieces of paper and pretend to be looking carefully at the pictures.

You will also need:
✦ An old wheelbarrow with metal objects for salvage;
✦ Some letters;
✦ A cash register for the shop – there are lots of toy ones around;
✦ Some 'food';
✦ A key;
✦ Tools for lock picks.

LAST-MINUTE TOUCHES

Your school may be lucky enough to have a stage with lights. If not, you could borrow two portable spot lights from a local secondary school or drama group.

Try to get a microphone on a stand – especially if some of your group have rather soft voices. After all this work you want the audience to hear you!

Make a programme for the audience. Look at some theatre programmes to find out how to set it out.

If you have included songs, type out the song sheet so the audience can join in.

AND FINALLY…

Make sure someone takes lots of photographs of you. Someone might even bring a video recorder along.

GOOD LUCK!

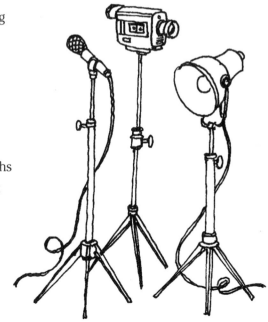

THE PLAY

The Evacuee

SETTING: In London and in Little Poppleton in Devon during the Second World War.

CHARACTERS:

- ✦ Albert Smith, a London boy
- ✦ Mavis Smith, his mother
- ✦ Harold Smith, his father
- ✦ George Aldridge, a boy from Devon
- ✦ Joan Aldridge, his mother. She runs the local shop.
- ✦ Thomas Field, George's friend
- ✦ Mrs Smedley, the billeting officer
- ✦ Mr Clifton, a member of the Home Guard
- ✦ Mrs Jarvis, a shopper
- ✦ Miss Watson, the teacher

There can be other non-speaking parts, for example: evacuees, villagers, local children.

SCENE 1

3 September 1939. The Smith family are in their dining room in London. They are sitting around the table listening to the Prime Minister talk on the wireless.

Harold turns off the wireless. There is silence.

MAVIS: Well, that's that then!

HAROLD: That's that, alright!

ALBERT: What? What? I don't understand?

HAROLD: Weren't you listening to Mr. Chamberlain, lad?

ALBERT: (*quickly*) Yes, I was. But I don't get it? He said at the end we were at war.

HAROLD: That's true. You see he told the jerries they mustn't march into Poland and now they've gone and done it. So it's war. It's not as though we haven't been expecting it – all the shelters and gas masks and such.

The air raid siren sounds outside.

MAVIS: (*screams*) Oh, my goodness! We're being bombed!

HAROLD: Quick – under here.

He grabs Mavis and Albert and pulls them under the table.

HAROLD: Now stay still. We'll be fine, you'll see.

MAVIS: What do we do?

HAROLD: Same as everyone else – help win this war. I'm off to join the army tomorrow – that new law said all us men have to. But you don't need to worry. The blokes down the pub were saying they reckoned it would all be over by Christmas.

MAVIS: Well that's a blessing. Maybe there's no point sending you off to the country, Albert.

HAROLD: You'll be right as rain. But don't forget to keep your gas mask with you all the time. Can't be too careful. I'll make this table into a decent shelter before I go. Get some wire down the sides like that leaflet showed us.

ALBERT: (*sounds upset*) I'll miss you Dad!

HAROLD: And I'll miss you – but we can write, can't we? And here – I'll tell you what – you can have my locksmith tools and look after them for me until I come back. They won't be any use here – we'll have to shut up the shop. How about that?

ALBERT: (*smiles broadly*) Really! That's great! I'll take ever such good care of them.

All Clear' siren sounds.

HAROLD: Listen to that – must have been a false alarm. I'm off
upstairs to get my stuff together.

They get out from under the table. Exit Harold. Mavis and
Albert clear the table.

SCENE TWO

September 1940. The dining room of the Smith's house
in London. Mavis and Albert are sitting at the table having
a meal. Mavis has a letter in her hand.

MAVIS: This letter is dated two months ago. Goodness knows where
your Dad is now! He didn't know about the bombing in
London when he wrote this. I don't think I'll tell him what
happened to those houses down the road. No sense in him
worrying about things he can't do anything about.

ALBERT: I hope it's all over soon. I hate carrying the gas mask
around. I hate having to blackout the house each night.
I hate the dark streets. It's even worse at school now because
so many kids went off to the country.

MAVIS: Yes, well that's another thing. Your Dad says he wants you
to go …

ALBERT: (*interrupts*) NO! I don't want to!

MAVIS: You've got no choice, I'm afraid. In any case I've decided to get work in one of the big factories making weapons. They need all the help they can get. I can't do that if I need to look after you.

ALBERT: That's not very nice – you sound as if I'm a bother. (*looks really upset*)

MAVIS: (*briskly*) Now, come on – you know that's not true. It's just that if we all help, the war will be over sooner and Dad will be home. I won't like being here by myself but we will both be happy that you are safe. It'll be great in the country – all that fresh air. You'll love it!

ALBERT: (*unconvinced*) I suppose so. I could write to Dad, couldn't I and then he wouldn't worry. I can write to you as well.

MAVIS: That's right. I'll find out where you can go tomorrow. Now eat up, it's nearly time for Tommy Handley on the wireless.

SCENE 3

Three days later. The High Street, Little Poppleton, Devon.

George and Thomas are sitting on the pavement outside the village shop. They are swapping cigarette cards.

GEORGE: You give me that one for these two – alright?

THOMAS: No. I want three for that one. It's a good one. I want him as well. He points to one of George's cards. They make the swap.

GEORGE: There's some more city kids coming. I heard someone in the shop say a train was getting in this morning.

THOMAS: Really? I thought we'd seen the last of them. Yours went home ages ago, didn't he?

GEORGE: Before Christmas. Reckoned it was safe in London. (*Says this proudly*) But I think I may have had a bit to do with it.

THOMAS: You were quite right. Can't have dirty, smelly city kids down here eating our food and pushing in where they're not wanted. Did your Mum ever find out?

GEORGE: No. She just thinks he missed his Mum – little cry baby!

THOMAS: Points down the road. Look. There's Mrs. Smedley. She's got a kid with her.

Mrs Smedley and Albert walk along the High Street. Albert has a suitcase and his gas mask. He is looking down at his feet all the time. She stops beside the boys.

MRS. SMEDLEY: Ah, George, dear.

George makes a face in Thomas' direction. Thomas laughs.

MRS. SMEDLEY: I'm so glad to see you. This is Albert. He's the same age as you so I expect he'll be in your class at school. There's been some dreadful bombing near his home so he's come here to be safe, haven't you, dear.

She pats Albert on the arm. He doesn't look up.

GEORGE: (*loudly*) Not very talkative is he! Is your Mum dead then?

Albert looks up, horrified

MRS. SMEDLEY: Now, now, George, dear. You must be kind to Albert.

George turns away from Mrs. Smedley and mouths 'WHY?' very clearly at Thomas.

Thomas laughs.

MRS. SMEDLEY: Is your mother in the shop?

GEORGE: Yes.

MRS. SMEDLEY: Ask her to pop out for a minute, dear.

George scowls, goes into the shop and comes out again with Joan.

MRS. SMEDLEY: Good morning, Mrs. Aldridge. This is Albert.

I've brought him to see you. I know your evacuee has gone home so you have a bed free. We need to find a home for Albert and so many people are full up.

JOAN: (*hesitates*) Well ...

MRS. SMEDLEY: It would be *so* kind of you. We've tried three places so far and had no luck. The poor boy will think that he's not welcome.

GEORGE: (*under his breath*) He's not!

MRS. SMEDLEY: What was that?

GEORGE: Nothing – but, I mean it's pretty cramped in our house.

JOAN: It's fine, Mrs. Smedley. He can have a bed in George's room. (*George looks furious.*) We would have had an evacuee anyway if poor Eric hadn't gone home. You're very welcome, Albert. We live above the shop here. I expect you'd like to help out a bit, like George does.

ALBERT: (*in a very quiet voice*) Yes. Thank you. Can I let my mother know I got here safely?

JOAN: Of course. You come in now and we'll sort out your bed. George has a desk in his room. You can write your letter there.

GEORGE: (*raises his voice*) But my models are on that!

JOAN: Then you must move them! Come in, Albert. Goodbye Mrs. Smedley.

MRS. SMEDLEY: Goodbye and thank you!

She walks off. Joan and Albert go inside the shop.

THOMAS: Bad luck!

GEORGE: Typical, isn't it. Plan B, I think. He won't last long.

They sort their cards. Then they freeze. Enter Mavis Smith to the side of the stage. She reads aloud from a letter.

Dear Mother,

The journey on the train today was alright. Thank you for the sandwiches. A lady called Mrs Smedley met the train. There were a few kids on it going to Little Poppleton. You wouldn't know you had got there. They've taken down all the signs in the country as well. Someone told me so I got off.

Mrs. Smedley took me round the village to find a home. I am with Mrs Aldridge. She runs the village shop. Mr Aldridge is away with the navy. I am writing this in my new room. I share with George. He is my age. I am sure I will like him a lot so don't worry about me. I will write again soon.

Love Albert.

Exit Mavis. Exit boys.

SCENE 4

Two weeks later. George and Albert are collecting salvage. Albert is pushing a wheelbarrow.

ALBERT: This is getting heavy!

GEORGE: (*grabs it off him*) No, it's not! You're just a weakling.

ALBERT: No, I'm not! Can't you ever think of anything nice to say?

GEORGE: Why should I? You're not my friend. You're just in the way but we all have to be kind to you because you've been 'evacuated'.

ALBERT: Let's just get on shall we? Look there's some cans and an old pan left for us. He picks them up and puts them in the barrow. It's funny to think they'll use this stuff in the factories isn't it? I mean, wouldn't it be great if my mother made guns and stuff out of the bits we collected today.

GEORGE: Oh, don't be so wet! That's not going to happen, is it?

Enter Thomas.

GEORGE: Oh, hey, Thomas! Bertie here thinks his mother will use this stuff in her factory!

Thomas laughs loudly.

ALBERT: Please don't call me Bertie. I don't like it.

GEORGE/THOMAS: (*imitating*) Please don't call me Bertie. I don't like it!

Albert grabs the barrow again and pushes on up the street.

Enter Miss Watson.

MISS WATSON: Hello, Albert. You're working hard.

George and Thomas run up to her.

GEORGE: Actually, Miss, it's our wheelbarrow, not his. He wanted to push it. Do you think Thomas and I will win the prize?

MISS WATSON: I don't know – but you've got a lot. We'll weigh it at school on Monday and see which group has won. Then we can send it off.

GEORGE: I bet it'll be Thomas and me.

ALBERT: What about me?

GEORGE: What do you mean? You didn't bring a barrow from London did you?

ALBERT: You know I didn't.

GEORGE: There you are, then.

MISS WATSON: Now, don't quarrel, boys. I thought we'd start work on a concert next week. What do you think about that? Can you sing or play an instrument, Albert?

George and Thomas pretend to choke with amusement. Albert looks upset.

ALBERT: Not really. What's it for?

MISS WATSON: Money for the war effort. It'll help people like your father. I'll tell you all about it next week. Keep up the collecting. Must go now. Goodbye.

BOYS: Goodbye, Miss.

Exit Miss Watson.

GEORGE: It won't help your father, Bertie. If you haven't heard from him I bet he's dead. Your father's written hasn't he, Thomas?

THOMAS: Oh, yes. I've had three letters. Your father will be dead by now, Bertie. Stands to reason.

ALBERT: (*shouts*) Shut up! Shut up! Shut up! That's a hateful thing to say. I don't say nasty things about your father.

He drops the barrow and runs off.

THOMAS: Well, that was a result! You should be rid of him soon at this rate.

GEORGE: Hope so. Hey, look who's coming!

Enter Mr Clifton.

GEORGE: Good morning, Mr Clifton. Are you off to fight the jerries?

MR. CLIFTON: I'll have none of your lip, young Aldridge. You have a bit of respect for us old'uns what fought in the last war. We've got a meeting up at the hall.

GEORGE: (*grinning cheekily*) Oh! A meeting! Very Important Home Guard Stuff. Are you going to practise marching and capturing the enemy?

MR. CLIFTON: My, you've a tongue on you! Why your mother don't box your ears for you, I don't know. You'll be glad we be doing the practising when the jerries come marching up from the coast.

THOMAS: Can we come and march?

MR. CLIFTON: No you cannot! You're collecting salvage, ain't you? Important that is. You get on with it and let the rest of us get on with what we're doing. Oh, and by the by – them bikes of yours.

THOMAS: What about them?

MR. CLIFTON: I see you in the village last night. You needs to cover more of them headlights. There should only be a slit of light in the middle.

GEORGE: We'll blame you when we bump into something because we can't see, then.

MR. CLIFTON: It's the same for everyone. You just have to go careful, like. Keep out of mischief for once in your lives!

Exit Mr Clifton.

GEORGE: My mother's been at the sewing again.

THOMAS: What's she making?

GEORGE: She's been cutting up some of her old stuff and making skirts and things. I'm worried she'll start on me next. These trousers are a bit tight. I'll end up with a pair with flowers on!

THOMAS: You can do a turn at Miss Watson's concert, then, can't you! Come on, let's get back and see what your evacuee is up to. Will he blub to your mother?

GEORGE: He hasn't yet. He's a tough nut to crack. But I'll do it!

They freeze on stage. Enter Mavis on one side of the stage and Harold on the other. They both have letters in their hand and read from them.

MAVIS: Dear Mother ...

HAROLD: I hope you get this letter ...

MAVIS: George and I went collecting salvage today ...

HAROLD: It was a lot of fun……..

MAVIS: I wonder if the metal from the pots we collected will go to your factory ...

HAROLD: At the weekend all the children from school are going to help at Newton's Farm.

MAVIS: They are really busy and there is too much for just the land girls to do so we are going over to help.

HAROLD: Everyone is really nice here and I have got lots of friends ...

MAVIS: Lots of love ...

HAROLD: Albert.

They both walk off. Boys on stage 'unfreeze' and walk off.

SCENE 5

**Two months later. Saturday morning inside the shop.
Joan is behind the counter. George and Albert are tidying
the shelves.**

Enter Mrs Jarvis.

JOAN: Good morning, Mrs Jarvis. How are you today?

MRS. JARVIS: Oh, fair to middling. Can't grumble. We heard from our
Frank yesterday. We don't know where he is but he sounds in
good spirits. He didn't say if he got the parcel we sent
earlier. I expect he'd moved on. What about John? How's he
doing?

JOAN: He's with the convoy in the Atlantic – you know, making sure
the supplies get through. It worries me to death because the
Germans will be after those ships, that's for sure. So John's in
the firing line, so to speak.

MRS. JARVIS: It's dangerous work, it's true, but everyone is pulling
together, that's the main thing. She turns to Albert. How's
your father getting on, dear? He's in the army, isn't he?

ALBERT: Yes, he was in France but I don't know where he went after
that. I've written to him ever so many times but I haven't
heard anything. I don't know if …

MRS. JARVIS: Now, you're not to fret, dear. Your father is doing a grand
job and the war will be over soon and you'll see him again.
Isn't that right, George?

GEORGE: Oh, yes, Mrs Jarvis. It'll be *so* nice when Ber ... Albert can
go home.

MRS. JARVIS: There! Isn't that nice! I bet you are glad you've made
some good friends here?

ALBERT: (*looks down at the floor*) Mmm.

**Mrs. Jarvis searches for her ration book. Albert pretends
to drop something and ducks out of sight so no-one
will see he is upset. George goes up to him.**

GEORGE: Oh, dear! Albert. You've got something in your eye. Let me
help.

ALBERT: (*whispers*) Push off!

GEORGE: (*pretends to be offended*) No need for that! I was only
trying to help!

JOAN: Boys, please get on with the tidying.

They go to different parts of the shop.

JOAN: Now Mrs Jarvis, what will it be?

MRS. JARVIS: I've got all our ration books here – so I'll take my butter, cheese and sugar for the week. We've run out.

Joan measures out the amount and wraps it in paper. As she is doing this Miss Watson enters.

MRS. JARVIS: I'd love some jam, I've got such a sweet tooth, but I really must try to save some rations.

MISS WATSON: Have you heard the recipes on the wireless? There was one for jam made from carrots.

MRS JARVIS: Well I never!

MISS WATSON: I tried it – not too bad – and at least we've plenty of carrots with all the vegetables everyone is growing. I put some carrots into a cake last night as we haven't any dried fruit at the moment. I haven't tasted it yet but it looks alright.

JOAN: The things we're getting used to! I'll tell you what I can't stand – that dried egg. I don't think I'll ever get the taste for those rubbery omelettes.

The other two ladies nod in agreement. Joan takes Mrs Jarvis' money, cuts off the coupons and hands the ration books back.

MRS JARVIS: Thank you. I'm on my way to the butcher now. Our Flo said he had some nice offal in.

JOAN: (*sounding excited*) Did he? I think I'll run along with you. George, you and Albert can mind the shop for a bit, can't you? If I'm not back at 12, lock the door for lunch.

Exit Joan and Mrs Jarvis.

MISS WATSON: Have you heard from your mother, Albert? You said you were expecting a letter.

ALBERT: Yes, miss. I got one today. She's coming to visit next week. She's still at the factory. They've put proper blackout up at all the windows so they don't have to keep putting it up and down all the time. Trouble is, she says, it gets really hot because they can't open the windows.

MISS WATSON: That must be most unpleasant. What does she do at the factory?

ALBERT: I'm not sure, really – it's to do with weapons. She said the foreman was really pleased with all the women. He hadn't thought they'd be any good but they are – good at fitting things into small spaces. She said having small hands helps.

MISS WATSON: Yes, I'm sure it does. Now, Albert, I want ...

GEORGE: (*interrupting*) I'll serve you, Miss. It's my mother's shop.

MISS WATSON: I think Albert …

ALBERT: (*interrupts her*) Oh, it's fine – I'm busy over here anyway.
He goes back to dusting shelves.

MISS WATSON: I'll have a loaf of bread, please.

GEORGE: We're very short today. Mother is selling half loaves.

MISS WATSON: That will have to do, then. And I'll take my cheese
ration. She hands over money and the ration book. George
wraps the food, cuts the coupon and gives back the change
and book. Goodbye. See you on Monday, boys.

Miss Watson exits.

GEORGE: We might as well lock up now.

ALBERT: But it's not 12 yet.

GEORGE: Mother will never know – she'll be talking to all her
friends in the butcher's queue.

**He goes over to the door, turns the sign to 'closed'
and pulls down the blind.**

GEORGE: I'd better lock the till – she always does that.

He locks the drawer of the cash register and puts the key in his pocket.

GEORGE: Now – let's see if you can get away from me. Chase you round the shop!

ALBERT: No!

GEORGE: Why? You chicken? Think I'll catch up with you too easily?

He runs at Albert and soon the boys are racing round the shop. Albert is trying to keep out of his way. This turns into a fight and they struggle on the ground.

Enter Joan from the door leading into the house.

JOAN: Thank you for ... What on earth is going on?! Get up at once! You spent all morning tidying and it looks as though you'll be doing it again this afternoon. Look at the state of the shop!

GEORGE: But ...

JOAN: No buts!

She goes back into the house and calls behind her.

JOAN: And take the envelope with the rent out of the till before you lock it. Mr Harris saw me at the butchers. He's coming

round at two. He said if we don't pay this month we're out. I
know he'll do it too. That so-and-so has been trying to get us
out for years. What will I tell your father? He'll never forgive me.

**George goes over to the cash register and feels in his pocket.
He can't find the key and spends a few minutes checking all
pockets.**

GEORGE: It's gone!

ALBERT: What?

GEORGE: The key! Didn't you hear my mother? We have to pay
the rent. She keeps it locked up in the cash register.
I bet I dropped it when you attacked me.

ALBERT: I didn't start it. Look, let's look around. I expect it's on the floor.

**Several minutes pass as the boys search every inch of floor
very carefully.**

GEORGE: It's no good. It's not here. There are so many cracks I bet
it's gone into a gap. I'm done for!

ALBERT: Why? Your mother can tell Mr Harris that the cash register
is stuck. He can have his money another day.

GEORGE: That might work for ordinary people. But believe me,
Mr Harris isn't ordinary! I'm going to be in *so* much trouble.

He carries on looking on the floor.

ALBERT: (*sounds excited*) I know. I have a way to help.

GEORGE: (*sneers*) What can *you* do?

ALBERT: You'll see.

He goes out into the house. George stands watching the door. He returns with his father's locksmith tools.

ALBERT: This will do the trick.

GEORGE: What is it?

ALBERT: A set of lock picks. My father had a business before the war. He opened locks if people had lost their keys and he also made new locks. It's fiddly. He had started to teach me and I'm looking after them until he gets home.

GEORGE: So your father is a thief!

ALBERT: How do you work that out?

GEORGE: He picks locks.

ALBERT: He opens them if someone has lost the key or it's all jammed up or something. Look – do you want me to do this or not? You could always go and own up.

GEORGE: No. No. You don't know my mother when she is really angry. You try – but I bet you can't.

Albert uses the tools and after a few minutes the drawer opens.

GEORGE: You did it! That's fantastic. Albert, you've saved my life. I'll get the rent money.

He removes an envelope from the cash register.

GEORGE: Now we can go and have our lunch.

ALBERT: What are you going to say about the key?

GEORGE: I don't know. What do you think?

ALBERT: We could tell her it was me. She won't get as cross with me, will she? I'll say that I locked up and dropped the key. We think it went into a crack in the floorboards.

GEORGE: Do you mind?

ALBERT: No. I've said so, haven't I!

GEORGE: You're alright, you are. A real pal. Tell you what. After we've tidied up this afternoon, what about going to call for Thomas and Fred and having a game of football?

ALBERT: I'd like that. Thanks, George.

The boys go into the house.

SCENE 6

May 1945. In Joan's kitchen. She is making food for the street party. George and Albert are helping.

JOAN: Do you know, I can't quite believe it's all over. I'm glad your mother said she'd come and celebrate the end of the war in Europe with us, Albert.

ALBERT: It was nice of you to ask her. She's very upset. We haven't heard from father for four years now – so I suppose he's not coming back. It will be really strange back in London without him.

GEORGE: You never know. He might be fine – just missing.

ALBERT: It's been really kind of you to have me to stay for so long, Aunty Joan.

MAVIS: Bless you, Albert. It's been a pleasure. We've all enjoyed it, haven't we George?

GEORGE: We certainly have!

ALBERT: You didn't when I first came.

GEORGE: (*looks embarrassed*) No, well I was a stupid kid, wasn't I? Can I visit you?

ALBERT: Yes, please. That would be great!

There is a knock at the door. Joan answers it. Re-enters with Albert's mother. Mavis and Albert run and hug each other.

MAVIS: I am *so* pleased to see you. Look what I've got. She takes an envelope out of her bag and hands it to Albert. He starts to read it silently.

ALBERT: (*shouts with delight*) He's coming home! He's been in a prison camp – but he's alright, AND HE'S COMING HOME!

JOAN: I am so happy for you, Mavis.

GEORGE: Great news! Both our fathers are safe.

ALBERT: It's over – and we've all got through! I don't think I will ever, ever forget all this – as long as I live.

GEORGE: Me neither.

They all hug.

THE END

GLOSSARY

Air raid warden a person who helped people to safety during bombing raids and checked that lights were not showing at night.

Air raid siren a noise that told people to get to a shelter because a bombing raid was about to start.

Allies the countries that fought against Germany.

Anderson shelter a shelter for up to six people, made of corrugated steel and sunk into the ground.

Billeting officer a person in charge of finding homes for evacuees.

Blackout when all windows were covered so no light could help the enemy planes.

Blitz Hitler's bombing of British cities. It is short for 'blitzkrieg' which is German for 'lightning war'.

Conscription compulsory service in the army, navy or air force.

Coupons these were cut out of ration books and allowed you to buy limited quantities of food, clothing and toiletries.

D-Day when allied troops landed on the beaches of Normandy in France and pushed back the Germans.

'Dig for Victory' a campaign to get people to grow food as much as possible.

Dunkirk landings the rescue of British soldiers from the beach at Dunkirk.

Evacuation the movement of people from towns to the countryside.

Gas mask a form of protection from a gas attack.

GIs American soldiers.

Huns a name that the British used for the Germans during the war.

Local Defence Volunteers older men who helped to make towns and villages safe. Also called the Home Guard.

'Make Do and Mend' using old items to make new or different ones.

Morrison shelter a shelter made of wire and mesh around a table.

Propaganda posters posters to give the public a special message.

Rationing a system to share out items that were in short supply.

Reserved occupation a job that was important for the war effort.

Salvage the saving of waste and scrap.

VE Day victory in Europe.

VJ Day victory over Japan.

Women's Land Army girls who worked on farms.

INDEX